WELCOM

Our Vacation Home Guest Book

Date of Arrival _____   Date of Departure _____

Guest Name_____

Hometown _____

Tips & Suggestions for Other Guests
_____
_____
_____
_____
_____
_____
_____
_____
_____

What Could We Have Done to Make Your Stay More Enjoyable
_____
_____
_____
_____
_____
_____

Additional Suggestions & Recommendations

Date of Arrival _____   Date of Departure _____

Guest Name _____

Hometown _____

Tips & Suggestions for Other Guests

_____
_____
_____
_____
_____
_____
_____
_____
_____

What Could We Have Done to Make Your Stay More Enjoyable

_____
_____
_____
_____
_____
_____

Additional Suggestions & Recommendations

Date of Arrival _____ Date of Departure _____

Guest Name _____

Hometown _____

Tips & Suggestions for Other Guests

_____
_____
_____
_____
_____
_____
_____

What Could We Have Done to Make Your Stay More Enjoyable

_____
_____
_____
_____
_____
_____
_____

Additional Suggestions & Recommendations

Date of Arrival _____ Date of Departure _____

Guest Name _____

Hometown _____

Tips & Suggestions for Other Guests
_____
_____
_____
_____
_____
_____
_____

What Could We Have Done to Make Your Stay More Enjoyable
_____
_____
_____
_____
_____

Additional Suggestions & Recommendations

Date of Arrival _____   Date of Departure _____

Guest Name _____

Hometown _____

Tips & Suggestions for Other Guests

_____
_____
_____
_____
_____
_____
_____
_____

What Could We Have Done to Make Your Stay More Enjoyable

_____
_____
_____
_____
_____
_____

Additional Suggestions & Recommendations

Date of Arrival _____ Date of Departure _____

Guest Name_____

Hometown _____

Tips & Suggestions for Other Guests

_____
_____
_____
_____
_____
_____
_____

What Could We Have Done to Make Your Stay More Enjoyable

_____
_____
_____
_____
_____

Additional Suggestions & Recommendations

Date of Arrival _____ Date of Departure _____

Guest Name _____

Hometown _____

Tips & Suggestions for Other Guests
_____
_____
_____
_____
_____
_____
_____
_____

What Could We Have Done to Make Your Stay More Enjoyable
_____
_____
_____
_____
_____

Additional Suggestions & Recommendations

Date of Arrival _____ Date of Departure _____

Guest Name _____

Hometown _____

Tips & Suggestions for Other Guests

_____
_____
_____
_____
_____
_____
_____
_____

What Could We Have Done to Make Your Stay More Enjoyable

_____
_____
_____
_____
_____

Additional Suggestions & Recommendations

Date of Arrival _____   Date of Departure _____

Guest Name _____

Hometown _____

Tips & Suggestions for Other Guests
_____
_____
_____
_____
_____
_____
_____
_____

What Could We Have Done to Make Your Stay More Enjoyable
_____
_____
_____
_____
_____
_____

Additional Suggestions & Recommendations

Date of Arrival _____   Date of Departure _____

Guest Name _____

Hometown _____

Tips & Suggestions for Other Guests

_____
_____
_____
_____
_____
_____
_____

What Could We Have Done to Make Your Stay More Enjoyable

_____
_____
_____
_____
_____
_____

Additional Suggestions & Recommendations

Date of Arrival _____ Date of Departure _____

Guest Name _____

Hometown _____

Tips & Suggestions for Other Guests
_____
_____
_____
_____
_____
_____
_____
_____

What Could We Have Done to Make Your Stay More Enjoyable
_____
_____
_____
_____
_____
_____

Additional Suggestions & Recommendations

Date of Arrival _____   Date of Departure _____

Guest Name _____

Hometown _____

Tips & Suggestions for Other Guests
_____
_____
_____
_____
_____
_____
_____
_____

What Could We Have Done to Make Your Stay More Enjoyable
_____
_____
_____
_____
_____
_____

Additional Suggestions & Recommendations

Date of Arrival _____   Date of Departure _____

Guest Name _____

Hometown _____

Tips & Suggestions for Other Guests
_____
_____
_____
_____
_____
_____
_____
_____

What Could We Have Done to Make Your Stay More Enjoyable
_____
_____
_____
_____
_____
_____

Additional Suggestions & Recommendations

Date of Arrival _____ Date of Departure _____

Guest Name _____

Hometown _____

Tips & Suggestions for Other Guests

_____
_____
_____
_____
_____
_____
_____

What Could We Have Done to Make Your Stay More Enjoyable

_____
_____
_____
_____
_____
_____

Additional Suggestions & Recommendations

Date of Arrival _____ Date of Departure _____

Guest Name _____

Hometown _____

Tips & Suggestions for Other Guests

_____
_____
_____
_____
_____
_____
_____
_____

What Could We Have Done to Make Your Stay More Enjoyable

_____
_____
_____
_____
_____
_____

Additional Suggestions & Recommendations

Date of Arrival _____   Date of Departure _____

Guest Name _____

Hometown _____

Tips & Suggestions for Other Guests
_____
_____
_____
_____
_____
_____
_____
_____

What Could We Have Done to Make Your Stay More Enjoyable
_____
_____
_____
_____
_____
_____

Additional Suggestions & Recommendations

Date of Arrival _____ Date of Departure _____

Guest Name _____

Hometown _____

Tips & Suggestions for Other Guests
_____
_____
_____
_____
_____
_____
_____

What Could We Have Done to Make Your Stay More Enjoyable
_____
_____
_____
_____
_____

Additional Suggestions & Recommendations

Date of Arrival _____   Date of Departure _____

Guest Name _____

Hometown _____

Tips & Suggestions for Other Guests
_____
_____
_____
_____
_____
_____
_____
_____

What Could We Have Done to Make Your Stay More Enjoyable
_____
_____
_____
_____
_____
_____

Additional Suggestions & Recommendations

Date of Arrival _____ Date of Departure _____

Guest Name _____

Hometown _____

Tips & Suggestions for Other Guests
_____
_____
_____
_____
_____
_____
_____

What Could We Have Done to Make Your Stay More Enjoyable
_____
_____
_____
_____
_____
_____

Additional Suggestions & Recommendations

Date of Arrival _____   Date of Departure _____

Guest Name _____

Hometown _____

Tips & Suggestions for Other Guests
_____
_____
_____
_____
_____
_____
_____
_____

What Could We Have Done to Make Your Stay More Enjoyable
_____
_____
_____
_____
_____
_____

Additional Suggestions & Recommendations

Date of Arrival _____ Date of Departure _____

Guest Name _____

Hometown _____

Tips & Suggestions for Other Guests

_____
_____
_____
_____
_____
_____
_____
_____

What Could We Have Done to Make Your Stay More Enjoyable

_____
_____
_____
_____
_____
_____

Additional Suggestions & Recommendations

Date of Arrival _____   Date of Departure _____

Guest Name _____

Hometown _____

Tips & Suggestions for Other Guests

_____
_____
_____
_____
_____
_____
_____

What Could We Have Done to Make Your Stay More Enjoyable

_____
_____
_____
_____
_____

Additional Suggestions & Recommendations

Date of Arrival _____ Date of Departure _____

Guest Name _____

Hometown _____

Tips & Suggestions for Other Guests
_____
_____
_____
_____
_____
_____
_____
_____

What Could We Have Done to Make Your Stay More Enjoyable
_____
_____
_____
_____
_____

Additional Suggestions & Recommendations

Date of Arrival _____ Date of Departure _____

Guest Name _____

Hometown _____

Tips & Suggestions for Other Guests
_____
_____
_____
_____
_____
_____
_____

What Could We Have Done to Make Your Stay More Enjoyable
_____
_____
_____
_____
_____
_____

Additional Suggestions & Recommendations

Date of Arrival _____ Date of Departure _____

Guest Name _____

Hometown _____

Tips & Suggestions for Other Guests

_____
_____
_____
_____
_____
_____
_____

What Could We Have Done to Make Your Stay More Enjoyable

_____
_____
_____
_____
_____
_____

Additional Suggestions & Recommendations

Date of Arrival _____ Date of Departure _____

Guest Name _____

Hometown _____

Tips & Suggestions for Other Guests

_____
_____
_____
_____
_____
_____
_____
_____
_____

What Could We Have Done to Make Your Stay More Enjoyable

_____
_____
_____
_____
_____
_____

Additional Suggestions & Recommendations

Date of Arrival _____ Date of Departure _____

Guest Name _____

Hometown _____

Tips & Suggestions for Other Guests

_____
_____
_____
_____
_____
_____
_____

What Could We Have Done to Make Your Stay More Enjoyable

_____
_____
_____
_____
_____
_____

Additional Suggestions & Recommendations

Date of Arrival _____ Date of Departure _____

Guest Name _____

Hometown _____

Tips & Suggestions for Other Guests

_____
_____
_____
_____
_____
_____
_____

What Could We Have Done to Make Your Stay More Enjoyable

_____
_____
_____
_____
_____

Additional Suggestions & Recommendations

Date of Arrival _____ Date of Departure _____

Guest Name _____

Hometown _____

Tips & Suggestions for Other Guests

_____
_____
_____
_____
_____
_____
_____

What Could We Have Done to Make Your Stay More Enjoyable

_____
_____
_____
_____
_____
_____

Additional Suggestions & Recommendations

Date of Arrival _____ Date of Departure _____

Guest Name _____

Hometown _____

Tips & Suggestions for Other Guests

_____
_____
_____
_____
_____
_____
_____
_____

What Could We Have Done to Make Your Stay More Enjoyable

_____
_____
_____
_____
_____

Additional Suggestions & Recommendations

Date of Arrival _____   Date of Departure _____

Guest Name _____

Hometown _____

Tips & Suggestions for Other Guests
_____
_____
_____
_____
_____
_____
_____
_____
_____

What Could We Have Done to Make Your Stay More Enjoyable
_____
_____
_____
_____
_____
_____

Additional Suggestions & Recommendations

Date of Arrival _____ Date of Departure _____

Guest Name _____

Hometown _____

Tips & Suggestions for Other Guests

_____
_____
_____
_____
_____
_____
_____

What Could We Have Done to Make Your Stay More Enjoyable

_____
_____
_____
_____
_____

Additional Suggestions & Recommendations

Date of Arrival _____ Date of Departure _____

Guest Name _____

Hometown _____

Tips & Suggestions for Other Guests

_____
_____
_____
_____
_____
_____
_____
_____

What Could We Have Done to Make Your Stay More Enjoyable

_____
_____
_____
_____
_____
_____

Additional Suggestions & Recommendations

Date of Arrival _____ Date of Departure _____

Guest Name _____

Hometown _____

Tips & Suggestions for Other Guests

_____
_____
_____
_____
_____
_____
_____

What Could We Have Done to Make Your Stay More Enjoyable

_____
_____
_____
_____
_____

Additional Suggestions & Recommendations

Date of Arrival _____ Date of Departure _____

Guest Name _____

Hometown _____

Tips & Suggestions for Other Guests

_____
_____
_____
_____
_____
_____
_____
_____

What Could We Have Done to Make Your Stay More Enjoyable

_____
_____
_____
_____
_____
_____

Additional Suggestions & Recommendations

Date of Arrival _____   Date of Departure _____

Guest Name _____

Hometown _____

Tips & Suggestions for Other Guests
_____
_____
_____
_____
_____
_____
_____
_____

What Could We Have Done to Make Your Stay More Enjoyable
_____
_____
_____
_____
_____
_____

Additional Suggestions & Recommendations

Date of Arrival _____ Date of Departure _____

Guest Name _____

Hometown _____

Tips & Suggestions for Other Guests

_____
_____
_____
_____
_____
_____
_____
_____

What Could We Have Done to Make Your Stay More Enjoyable

_____
_____
_____
_____
_____

Additional Suggestions & Recommendations

Date of Arrival _____   Date of Departure _____

Guest Name _____

Hometown _____

Tips & Suggestions for Other Guests
_____
_____
_____
_____
_____
_____
_____

What Could We Have Done to Make Your Stay More Enjoyable
_____
_____
_____
_____
_____
_____

Additional Suggestions & Recommendations

Date of Arrival _____   Date of Departure _____

Guest Name _____

Hometown _____

Tips & Suggestions for Other Guests
_____
_____
_____
_____
_____
_____
_____
_____

What Could We Have Done to Make Your Stay More Enjoyable
_____
_____
_____
_____
_____

Additional Suggestions & Recommendations

Date of Arrival _____   Date of Departure _____

Guest Name _____

Hometown _____

Tips & Suggestions for Other Guests
_____
_____
_____
_____
_____
_____
_____
_____

What Could We Have Done to Make Your Stay More Enjoyable
_____
_____
_____
_____
_____
_____

Additional Suggestions & Recommendations

Date of Arrival _____ Date of Departure _____

Guest Name _____

Hometown _____

Tips & Suggestions for Other Guests

_____
_____
_____
_____
_____
_____
_____
_____

What Could We Have Done to Make Your Stay More Enjoyable

_____
_____
_____
_____
_____
_____

Additional Suggestions & Recommendations

Date of Arrival _____   Date of Departure _____

Guest Name _____

Hometown _____

Tips & Suggestions for Other Guests
_____
_____
_____
_____
_____
_____
_____
_____

What Could We Have Done to Make Your Stay More Enjoyable
_____
_____
_____
_____
_____

Additional Suggestions & Recommendations

Date of Arrival _____ Date of Departure _____

Guest Name _____

Hometown _____

Tips & Suggestions for Other Guests
_____
_____
_____
_____
_____
_____
_____

What Could We Have Done to Make Your Stay More Enjoyable
_____
_____
_____
_____
_____

Additional Suggestions & Recommendations

Date of Arrival _____   Date of Departure _____

Guest Name _____

Hometown _____

Tips & Suggestions for Other Guests
_____
_____
_____
_____
_____
_____
_____
_____

What Could We Have Done to Make Your Stay More Enjoyable
_____
_____
_____
_____
_____
_____

Additional Suggestions & Recommendations

Date of Arrival _____   Date of Departure _____

Guest Name _____

Hometown _____

Tips & Suggestions for Other Guests

_____
_____
_____
_____
_____
_____
_____
_____

What Could We Have Done to Make Your Stay More Enjoyable

_____
_____
_____
_____
_____

Additional Suggestions & Recommendations

Date of Arrival _____   Date of Departure _____

Guest Name _____

Hometown _____

Tips & Suggestions for Other Guests
_____
_____
_____
_____
_____
_____
_____
_____
_____

What Could We Have Done to Make Your Stay More Enjoyable
_____
_____
_____
_____
_____
_____

Additional Suggestions & Recommendations

Date of Arrival _____ Date of Departure _____

Guest Name_____

Hometown _____

Tips & Suggestions for Other Guests
_____
_____
_____
_____
_____
_____
_____
_____

What Could We Have Done to Make Your Stay More Enjoyable
_____
_____
_____
_____
_____
_____

Additional Suggestions & Recommendations

Date of Arrival _____ Date of Departure _____

Guest Name _____

Hometown _____

Tips & Suggestions for Other Guests

_____
_____
_____
_____
_____
_____
_____
_____

What Could We Have Done to Make Your Stay More Enjoyable

_____
_____
_____
_____
_____
_____

Additional Suggestions & Recommendations

Date of Arrival _____ Date of Departure _____

Guest Name _____

Hometown _____

Tips & Suggestions for Other Guests

_____

What Could We Have Done to Make Your Stay More Enjoyable

_____

Additional Suggestions & Recommendations

Date of Arrival _____ Date of Departure _____

Guest Name _____

Hometown _____

Tips & Suggestions for Other Guests
_____
_____
_____
_____
_____
_____
_____
_____

What Could We Have Done to Make Your Stay More Enjoyable
_____
_____
_____
_____
_____
_____

Additional Suggestions & Recommendations

Date of Arrival _____ Date of Departure _____

Guest Name _____

Hometown _____

Tips & Suggestions for Other Guests

_____
_____
_____
_____
_____
_____
_____
_____

What Could We Have Done to Make Your Stay More Enjoyable

_____
_____
_____
_____
_____
_____

Additional Suggestions & Recommendations

www.ingramcontent.com/pod-product-compliance
Lightning Source LLC
LaVergne TN
LVHW080940190125
801667LV00012B/1395